MW01644283

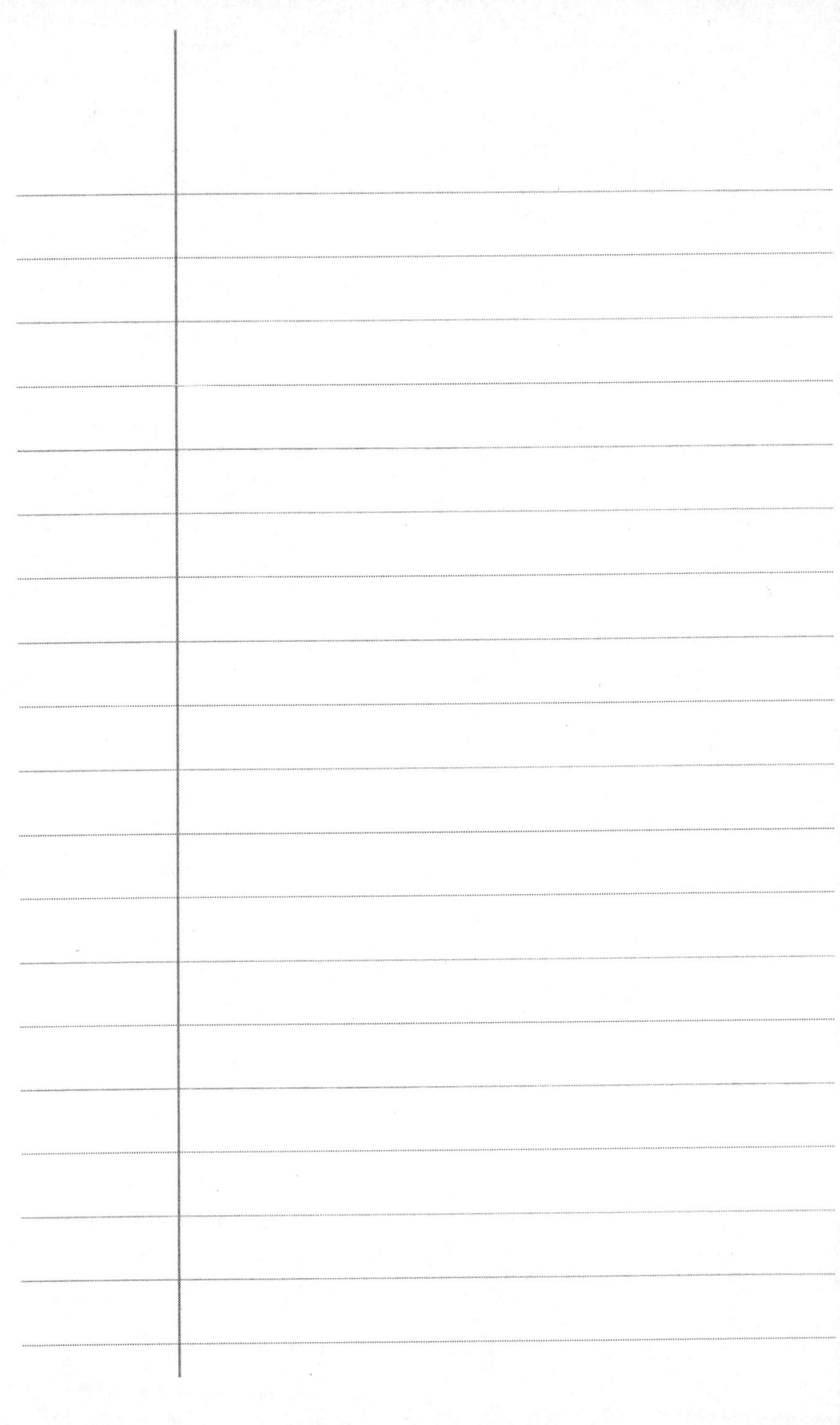

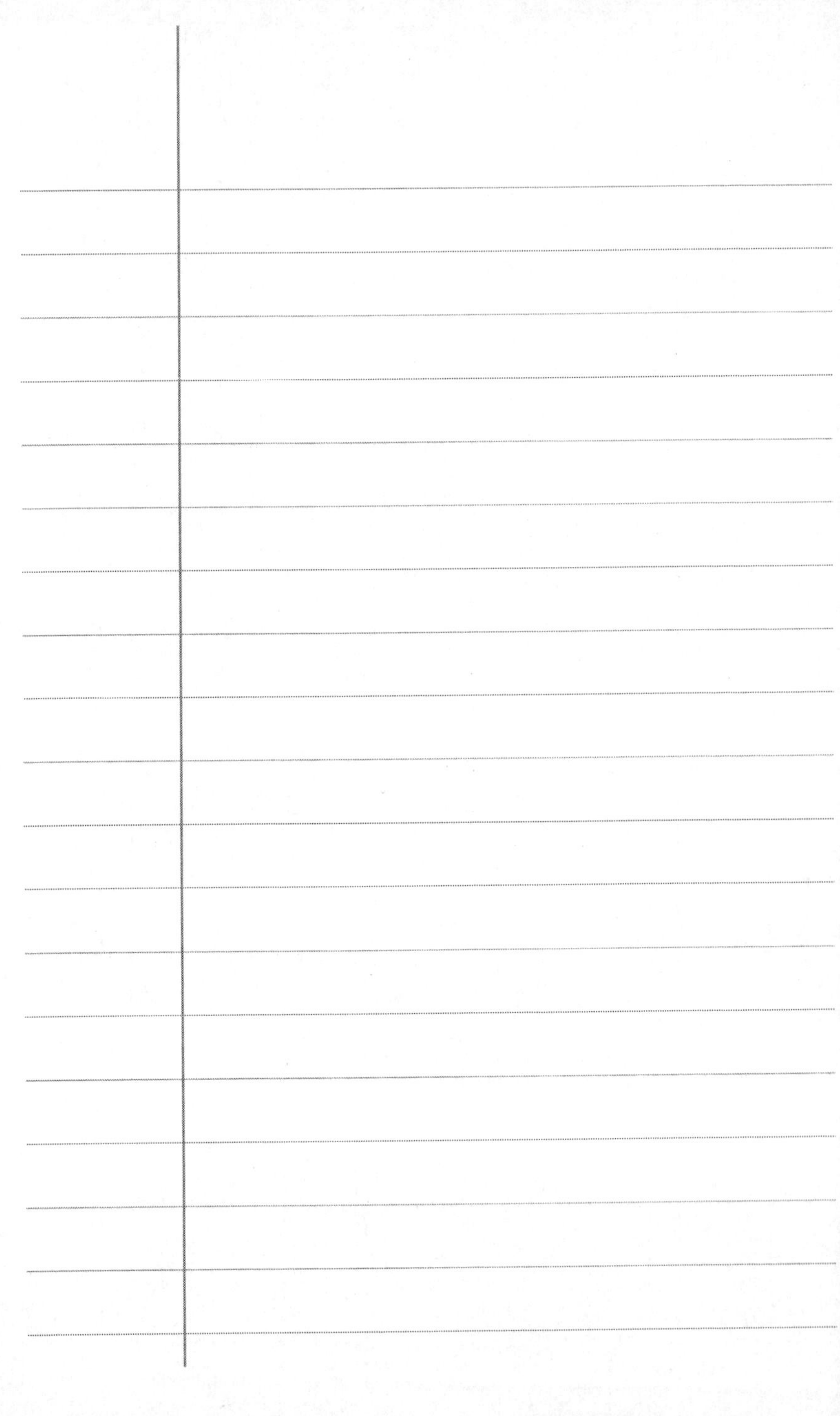

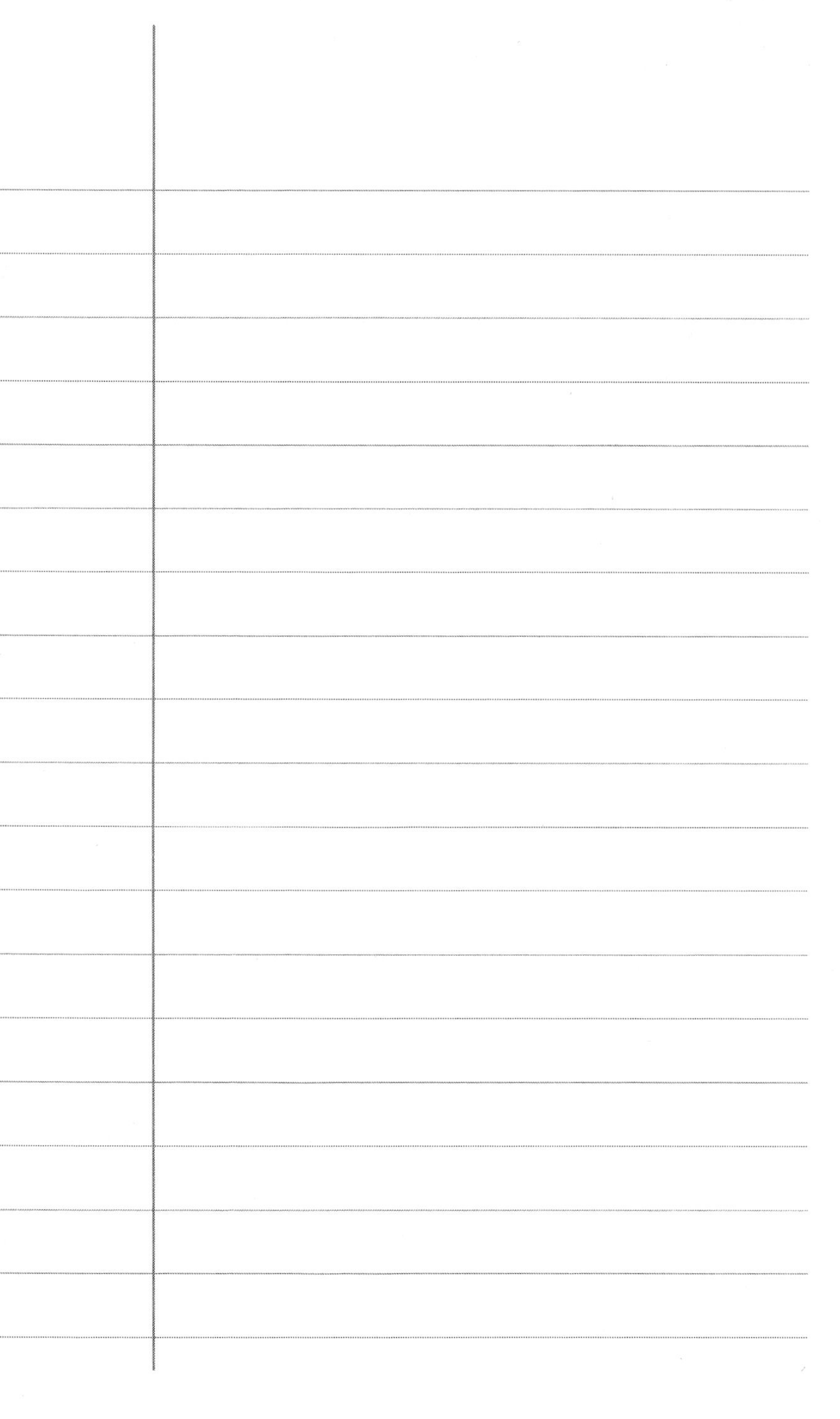

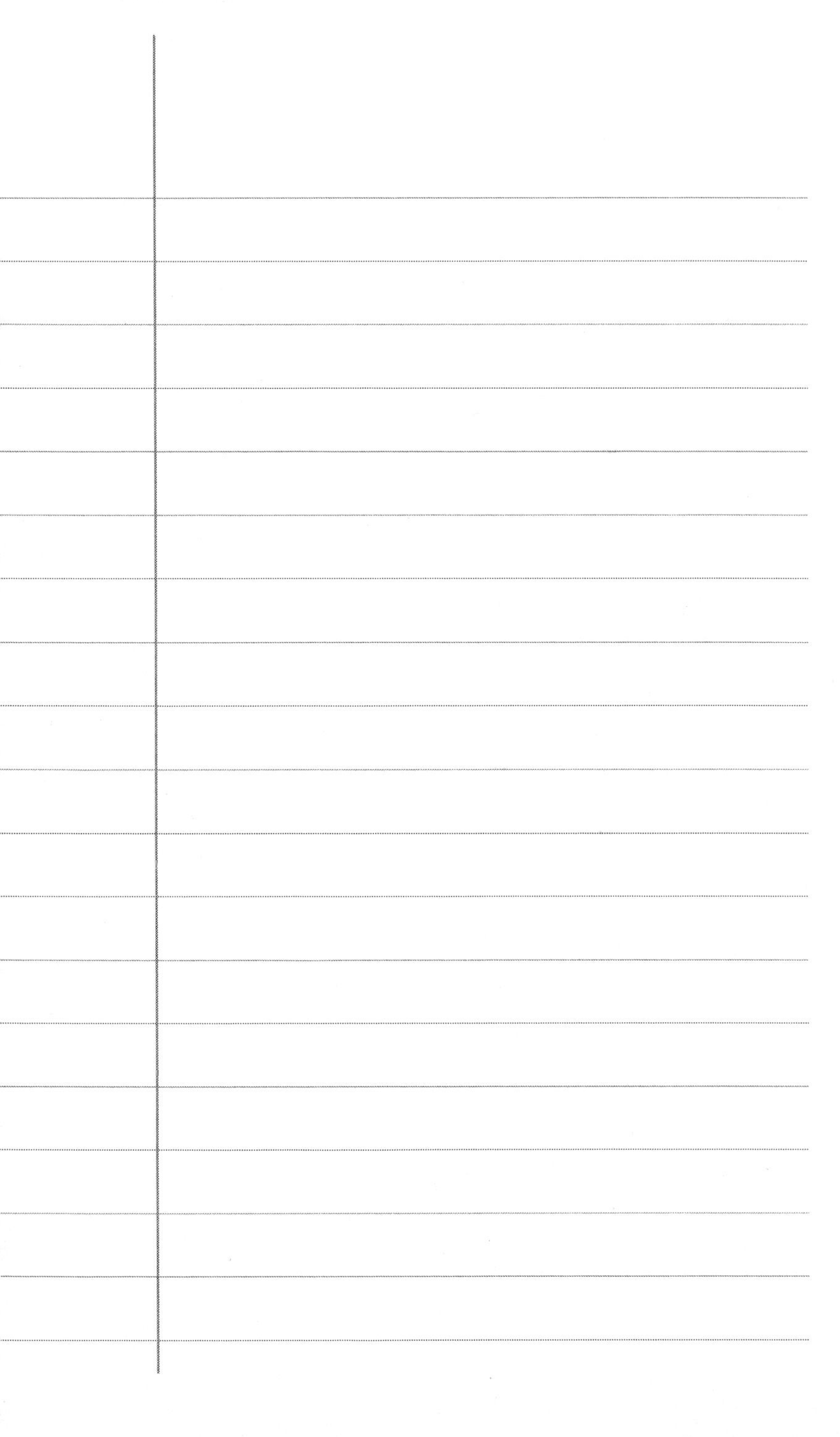

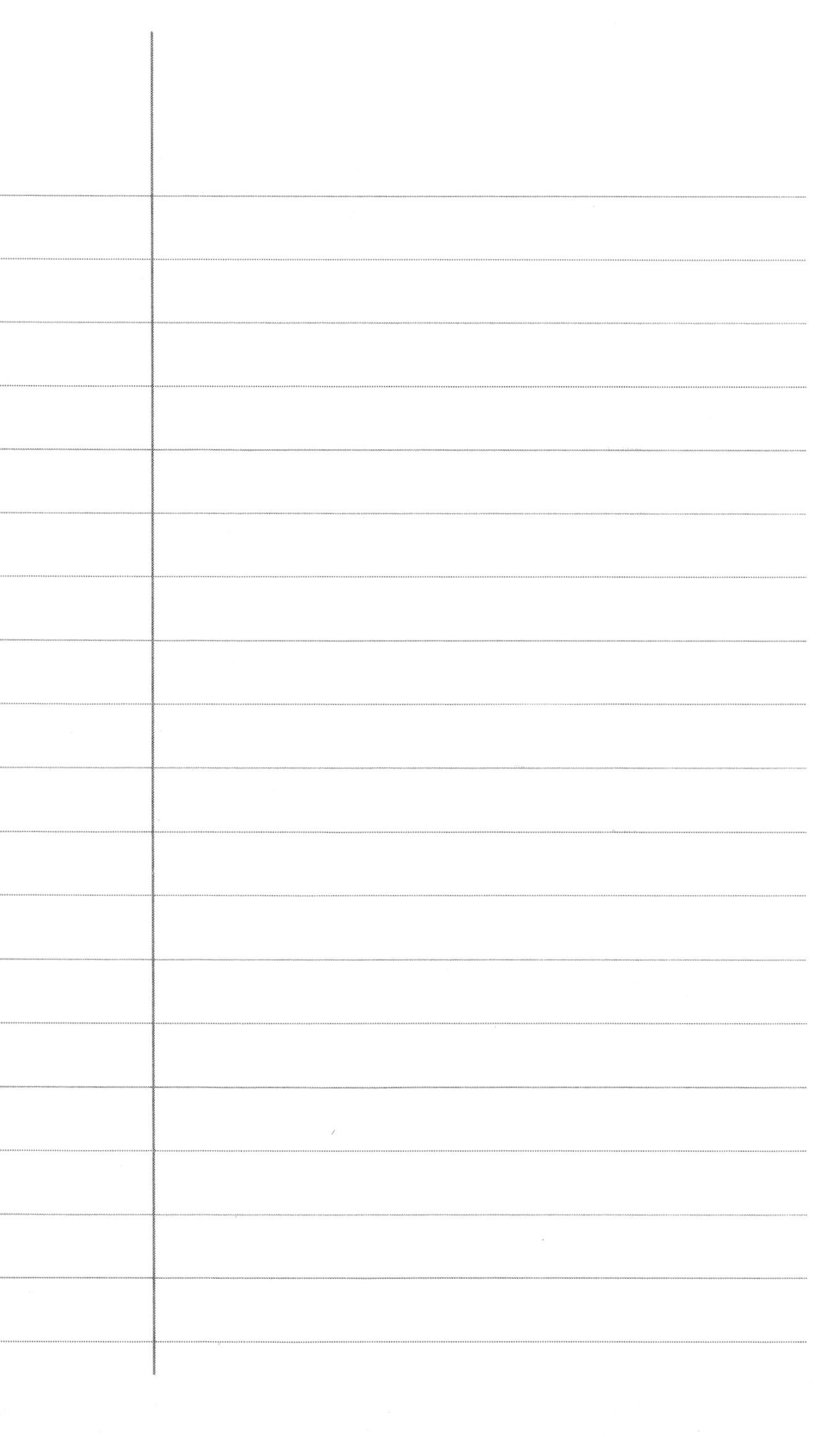

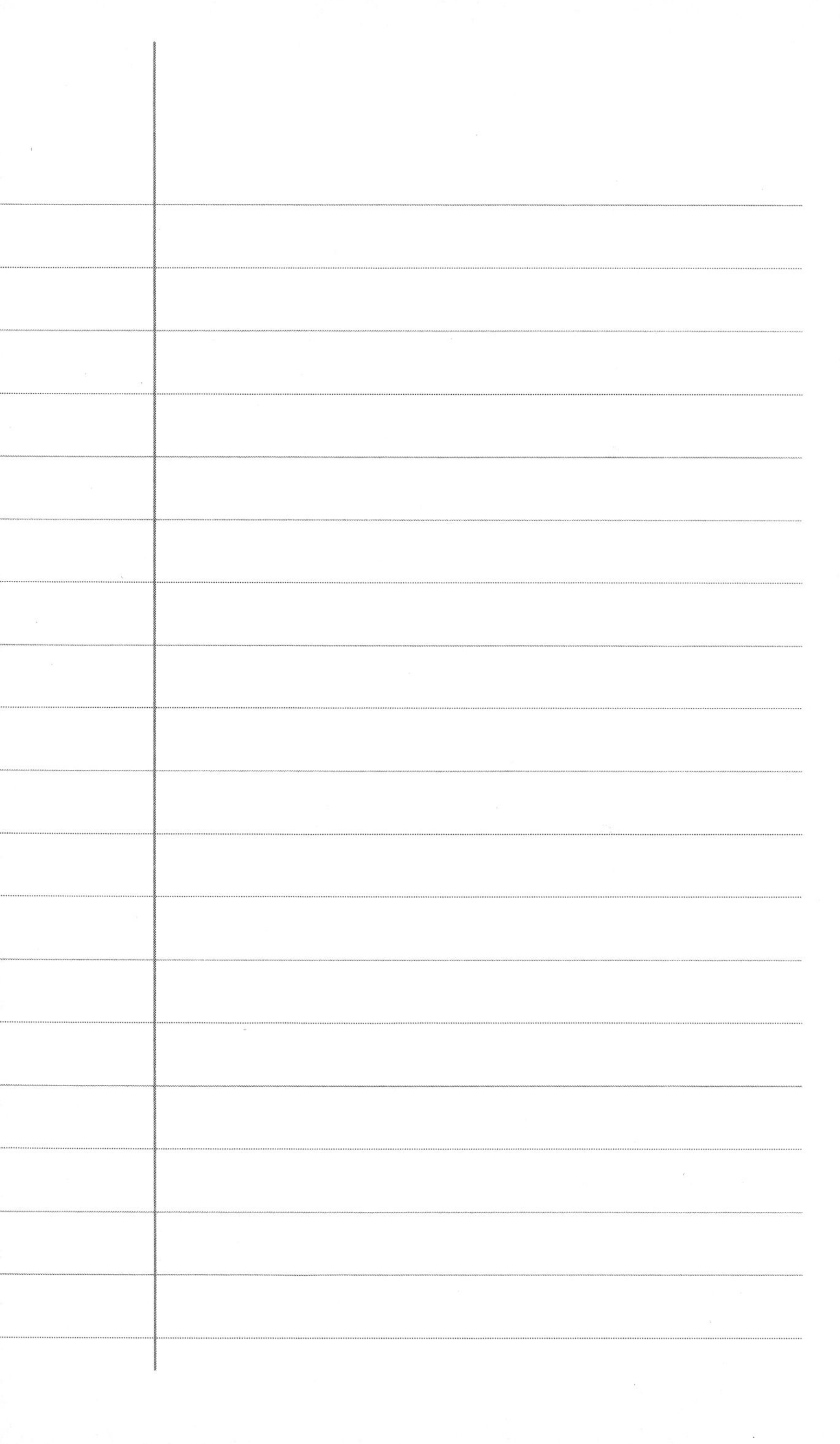

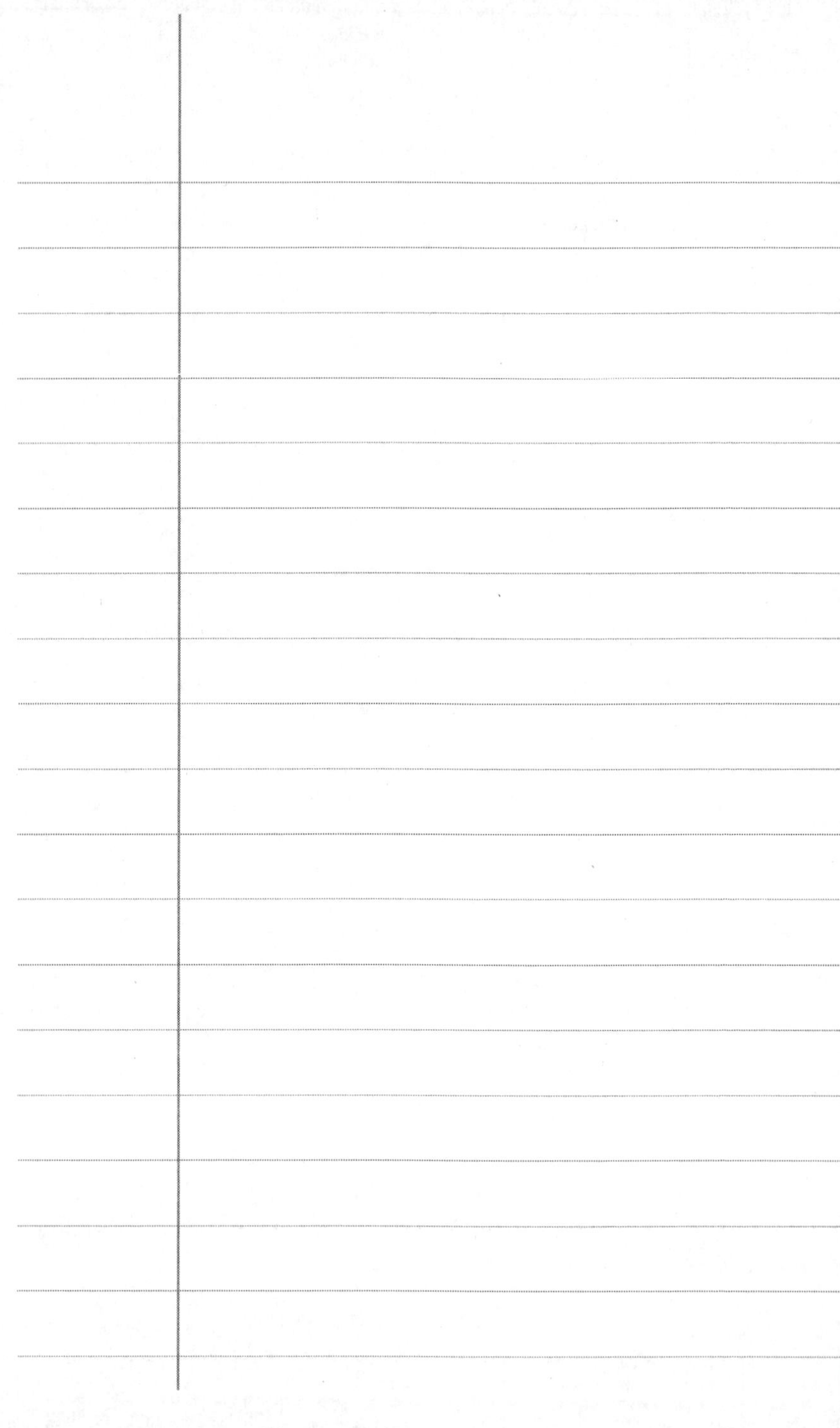

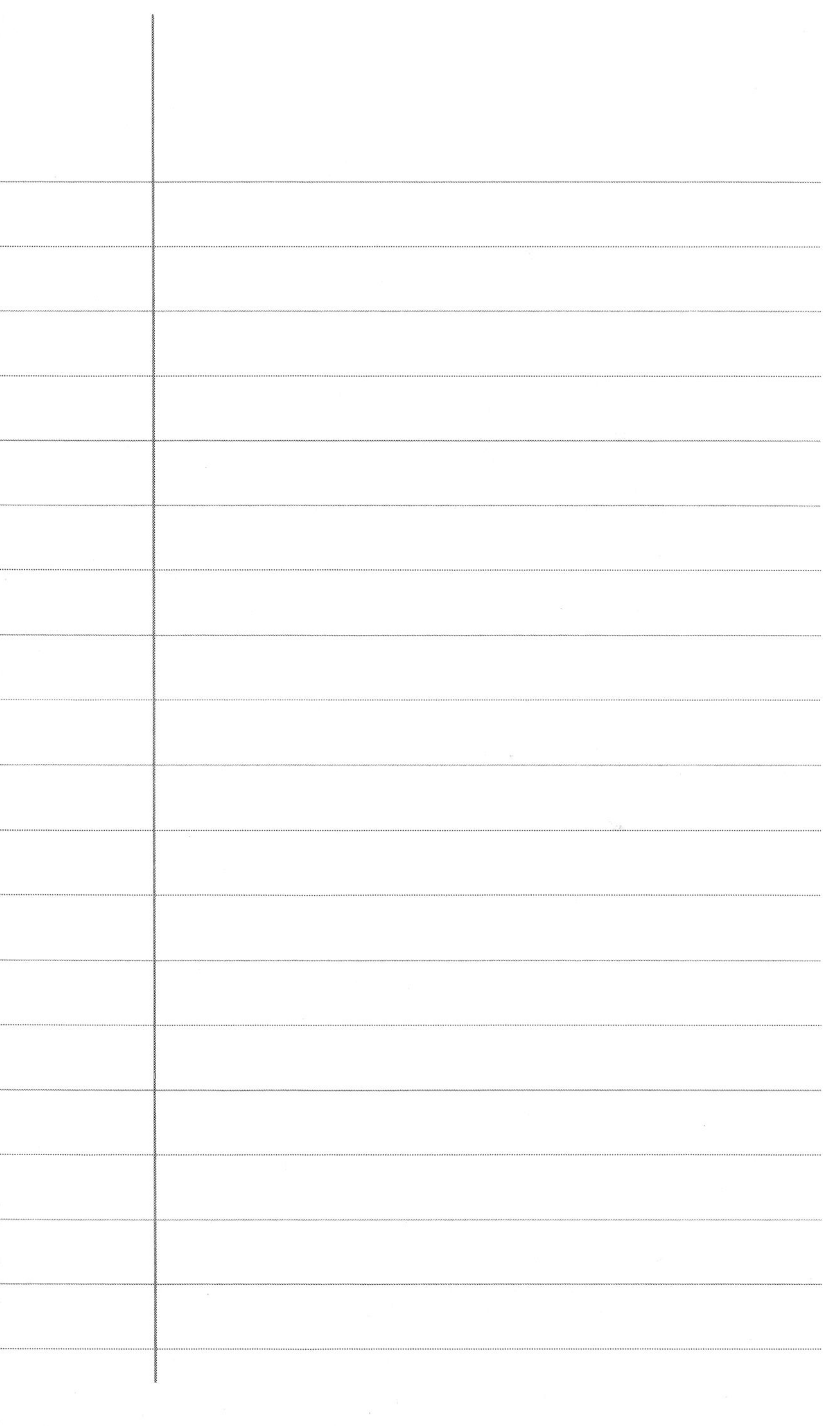

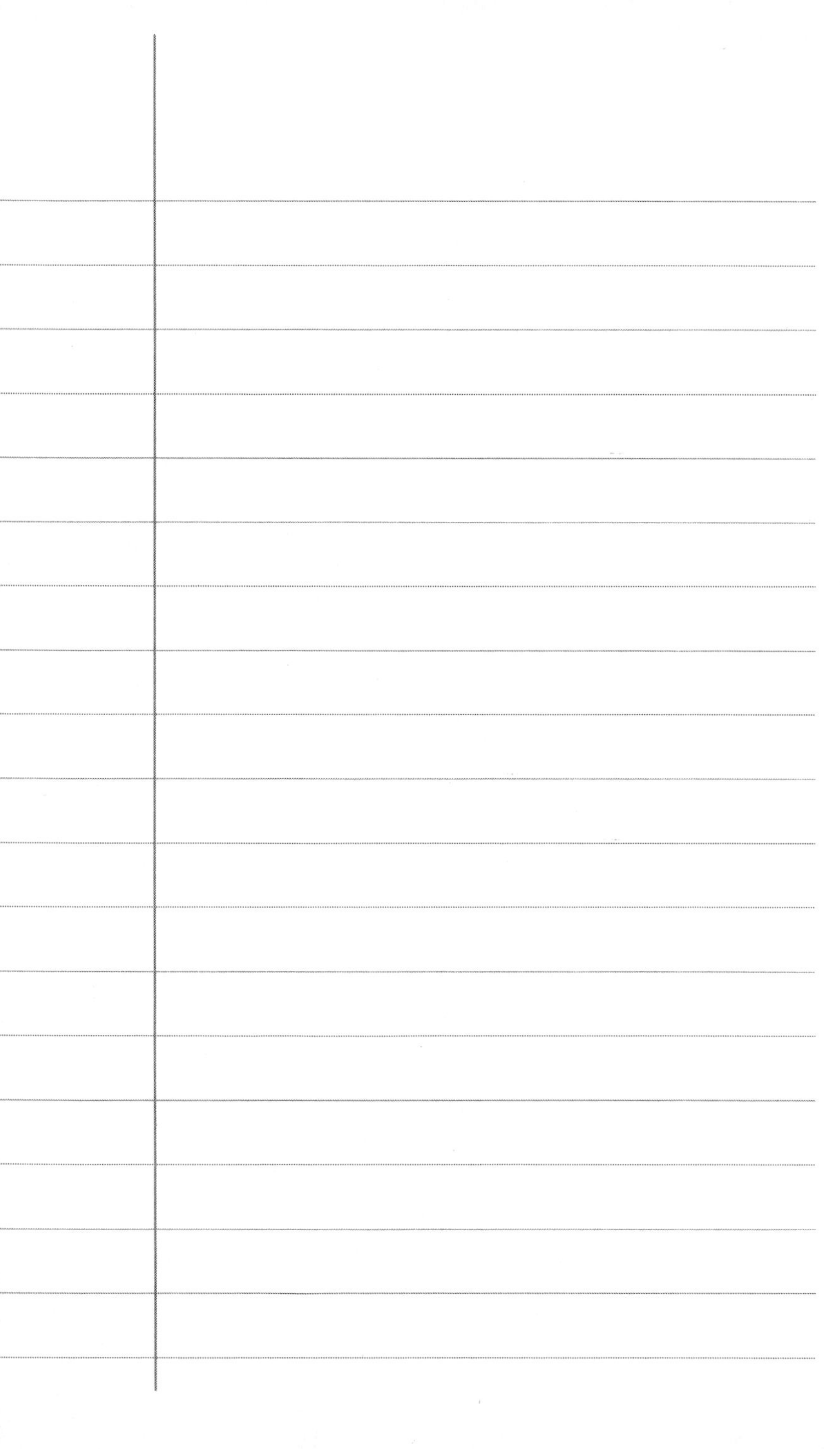

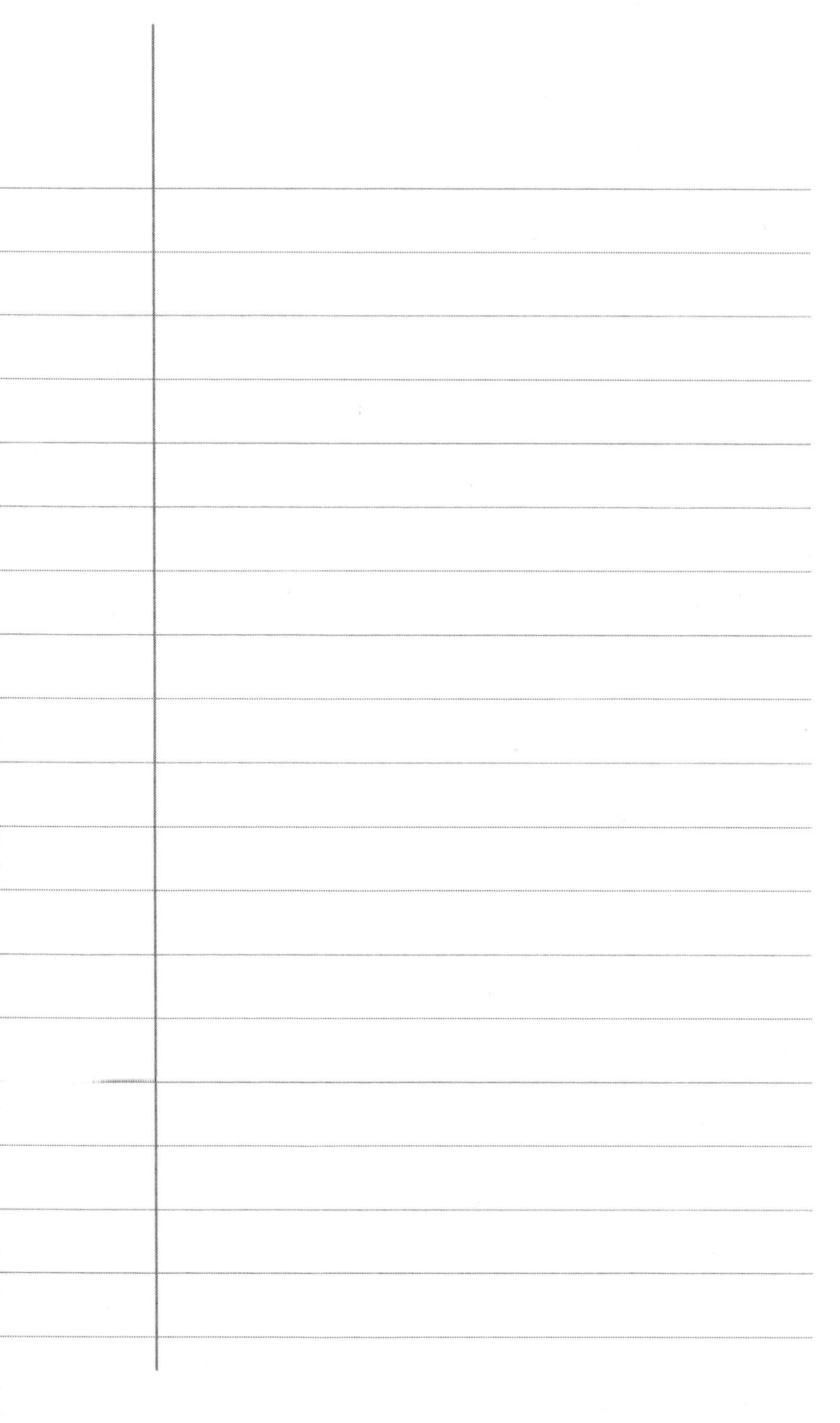

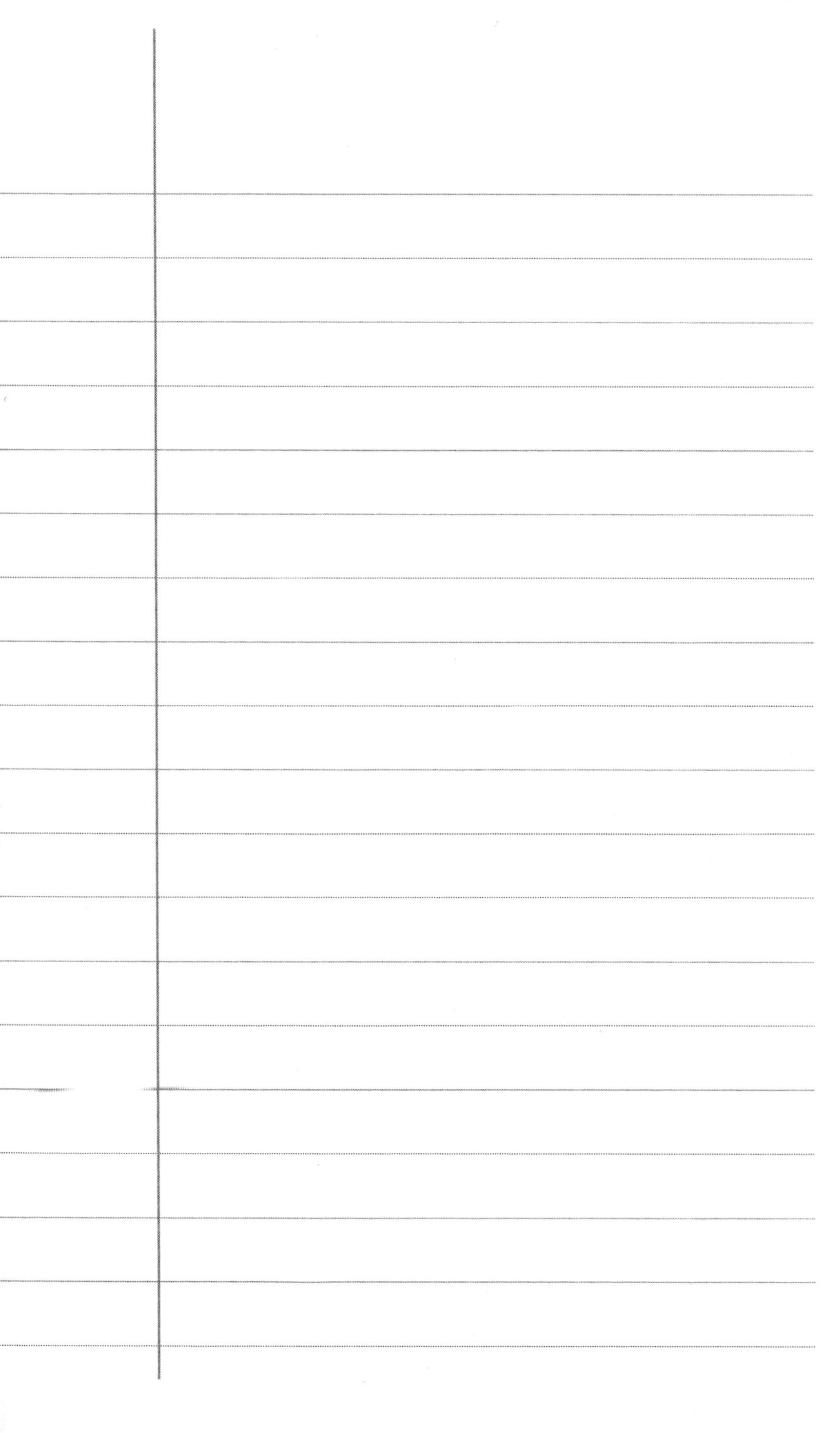

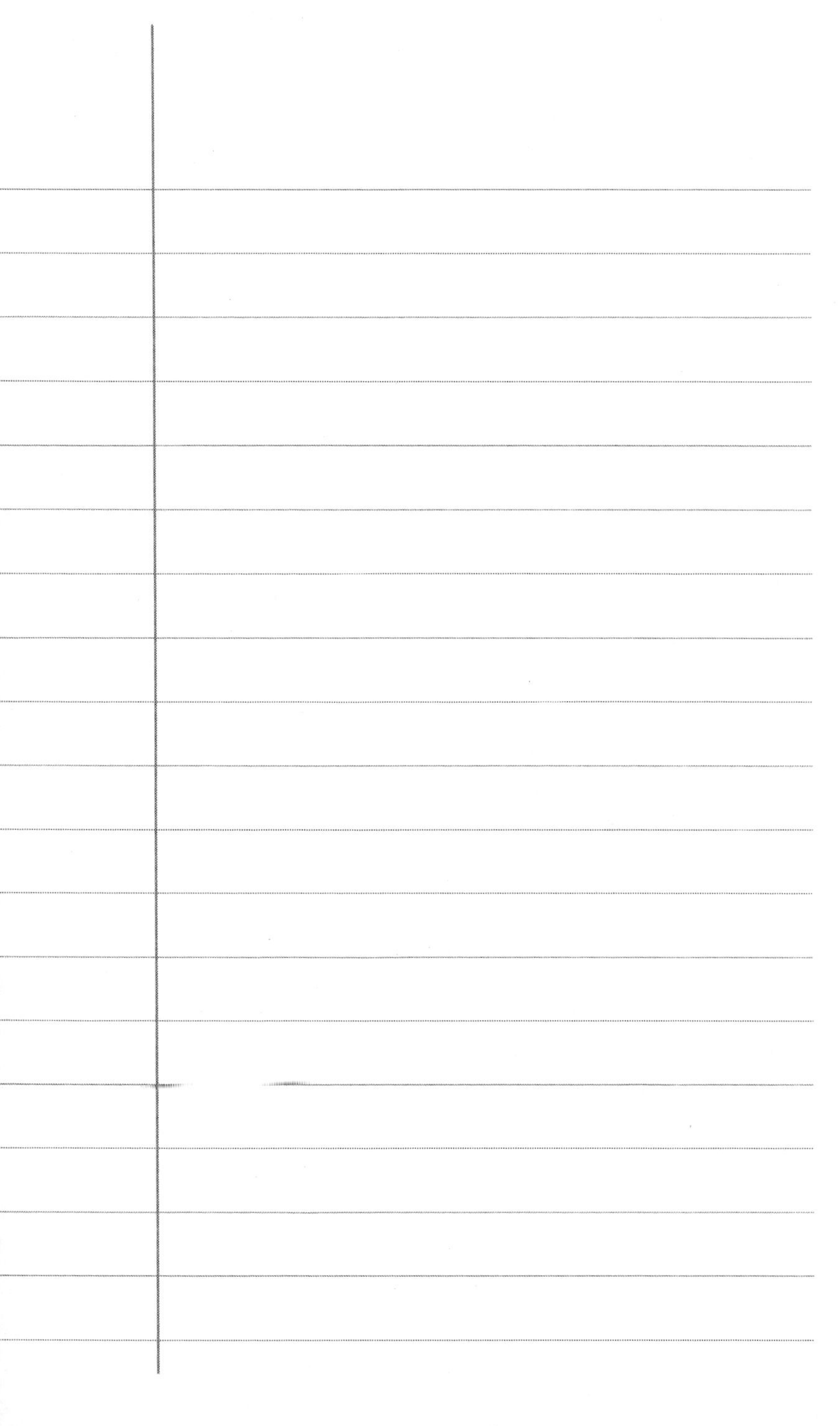

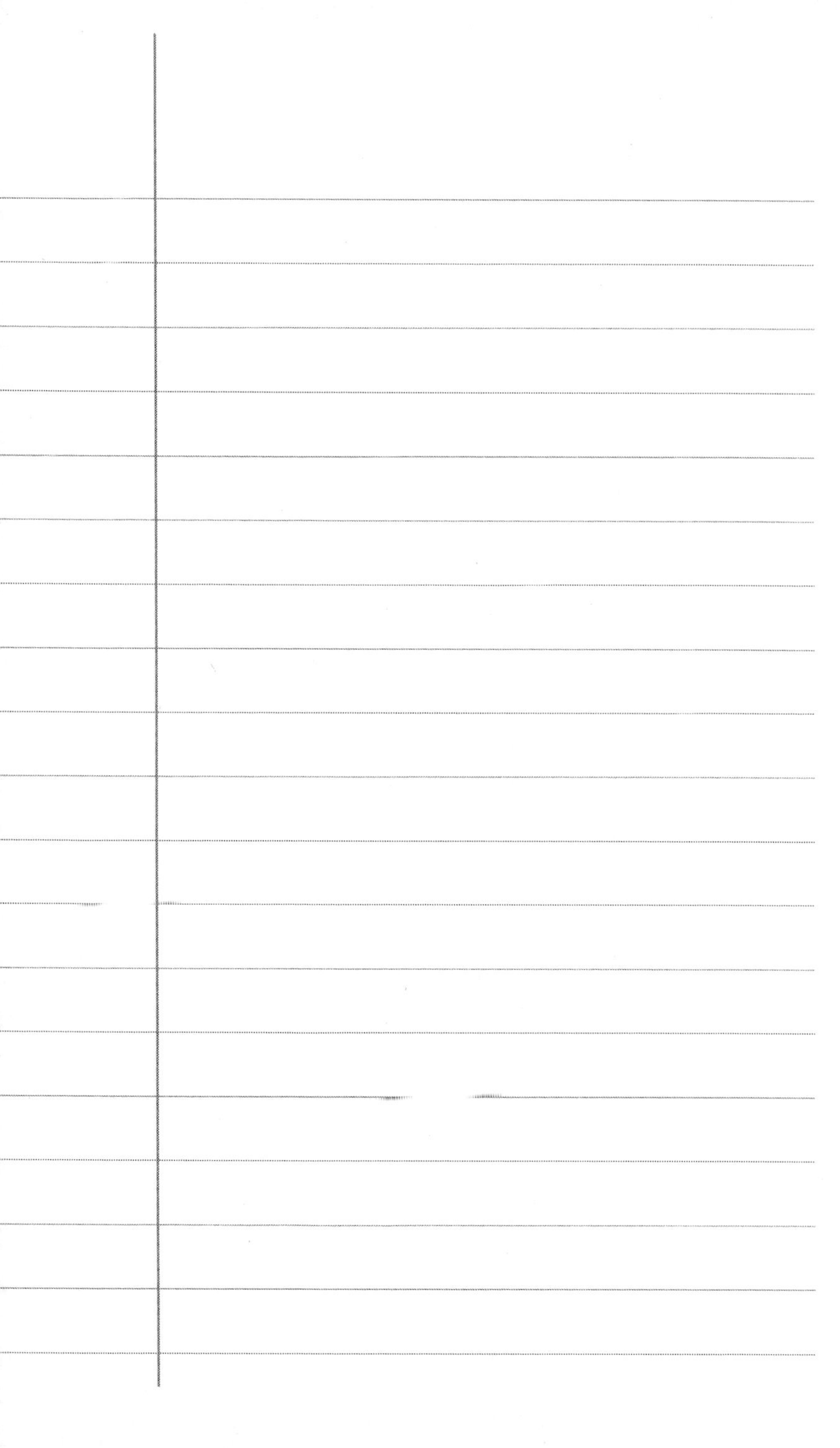

Made in the USA
Columbia, SC
02 July 2025

60255194R00057